GOING PLACES

Victor Hugo Green and His Glorious Book

Written by **Tonya Bolden** ◆ Illustrated by **Eric Velasquez**

Quill Tree Books
An Imprint of HarperCollinsPublishers

Once described as "tall, well-built, always impeccably groomed," Victor Hugo Green seemed to walk about with sunshine inside.

And plenty of pride.

What's more, he "not only believed in facing a problem, but also in doing something about it."

That's from a New York newspaper's travel section called "Going Places!"

And don't you know, Victor Hugo Green had *great* get-up-and-go!

That great get-up-and-go must have made Victor Hugo Green a
prime wonder at his good, steady job. It had him on the move *a lot*.

In a sharp blue-gray uniform,
bell crown cap, perhaps, upon his head,
and with a big (some days bulging, no doubt) satchel over a shoulder,
he likely stepped lively
up and down
New Jersey streets,
first in Hackensack,
then in nearby little Leonia.

One, two, and more days a week, Victor Hugo Green
flipped open mailboxes and
rang doorbells,
bearing
packages (large and small),
letters (thick and thin),
magazines, catalogs, along with—ugh!—bills, and . . .
I'm guessing postcards too.

Maybe from faraway places like France, where he had served the United States as a soldier during World War I.

Maybe from cities within the States like . . .
The Windy City,
The City of Angels,
or Beantown.

Perhaps also from the bustling Motor City.

Victor Hugo Green kept delivering mail in little Leonia after he and his lovely wife, Alma, moved across the Hudson River to the city where he was born.

There, in the Big Apple, the couple made a home in Harlem, with its world of Black folks.

Cooks, carpenters, clerks,
teachers, preachers,
actors, entrepreneurs, and
Augusta Savage, sculptor in bronze, in plaster, in clay, in marble;
travel-loving Langston Hughes, much-applauded poet;
dapper Duke Ellington, bandleader, composer;
trailblazing Dr. May Edward Chinn.

Harlem was soon home to brainy, backslapping Thurgood Marshall,
civil rights attorney.

Such folks were keeping their chins up during these days of the Great Depression, when a lot of businesses—ice-cream shops to clothing stores—closed, when so many people lost jobs in the Windy City, the City of Angels, Beantown, in other cities too.

As for the Motor City, it sputtered along, producing sedans, roadsters, phaetons, coupes, and cabriolets.

With more highways and turnpikes being built, with smart automakers slashing prices and shifting gears to less costly models, heaps of Americans were going places behind the wheels of their very own new or like-new motorcars.

TRAVELING JIM CROW

BY GEORGE S. SCHUYLER

Hence, all Negroes who can do so purchase an automobile as soon as possible in order to be free of discomfort, discrimination, segregation and insult.
 —George S. Schuyler,
"Traveling Jim Crow" (1930),
about ordeals Black people
faced when traveling by train.

These travelers were cooks, carpenters, clerks,
teachers, preachers,
actors, entrepreneurs, and
Augusta Savages,
Langston Hugheses,
Duke Ellingtons,
Dr. May Edward Chinns,
Thurgood Marshalls, and . . .
Victor Hugo Greens.

Traveling on business to Boston or Baltimore,
to Chicago or Charlotte for conferences, conventions,
to weddings, graduations, family reunions
in Rock Hill, Rockaway, or Richmond.

Traveling to all sorts of places, some of them resorts.

Like the Bay State's Oak Bluffs on Martha's Vineyard.
Like Idlewild, the Great Lakes State's "Black Eden."
Like Chesapeake Bay's Highland Beach, founded by Laura Douglass
and her husband, Charles (a son of Frederick Douglass).

People made sad trips too.

Mama, Papa, Big Sis, Little Brother, a cousin,
an auntie, or an uncle was doing poorly.
Grandma or Grandpa had passed on.

These travelers,
whether going places with smiles
or with tears in their eyes,
could face
hassles, humiliations, hardships.
Even bodily harm.

Because Jim Crow—segregation—was intense in the North, South, East, and West.
Because legions refused to see Black people's humanity.
People had to worry about sundown towns too.

In sundown towns, Black people may have been free to walk about when the sun was out to, say, deliver goods, or to work as a maid or in a mechanic's shop, but . . .

come nightfall—

NO COLOREDS AFTER DARK

So read a sign one man recalled seeing in an Illinois town for years.

Going places could be especially trying
for those most frequent of Black travelers, like
catchers, pitchers,
basemen, fielders

for the Philadelphia Stars,
the Kansas City Monarchs,
the Homestead Grays.

Duke Ellington and other great
(and not-so-great) entertainers were
sometimes on the road for *weeks*.

The troubles of traveling while Black were not new. And Black people were not clueless about what to do when going places.

They used their brains to navigate unfriendly, hostile, dangerous terrain.

Thanks to ads and articles in Black-owned newspapers—
the *Pittsburgh Courier*, the *Chicago Defender*, the *Louisville Leader*,
the *Call and Post* in Cleveland,
the *New York Age*,
the *New York Amsterdam News*—
they made maps in their minds
of safe, happy-to-serve-you! places
to stretch their legs,
get a good night's sleep,
grab a cup of coffee, a chicken and waffles dish, a cheeseburger, or
partake of a five-course feast!

Through word of mouth they learned about sundown towns
and how best to steer clear of them.

Victor Hugo Green was really vexed by the problems he and his people could face when going places. Inspired by earlier guides, including ones with Black travelers in mind, he got busy problem-solving!

From the grapevine he grabbed goo-gobs of information.

He pored over newspaper ads and articles.

He tapped his fellow blue-gray-garbed brothers for tips.

Super sleuth Victor Hugo Green then fashioned his findings into a book.

And it became a highly prized guide,
known far and wide
as the *Green Book*.

The *Green Book* started off small in 1936.

Just a pamphlet.

Just listings of welcoming places in New York City and nearby towns.

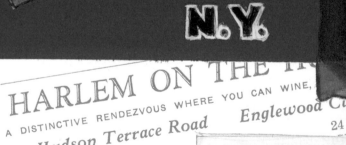

But two years on, the *Green Book*—25 cents a copy—was more than twenty pages long, listing safe, welcoming places in large cities east of the Mississippi River.

And it kept growing.

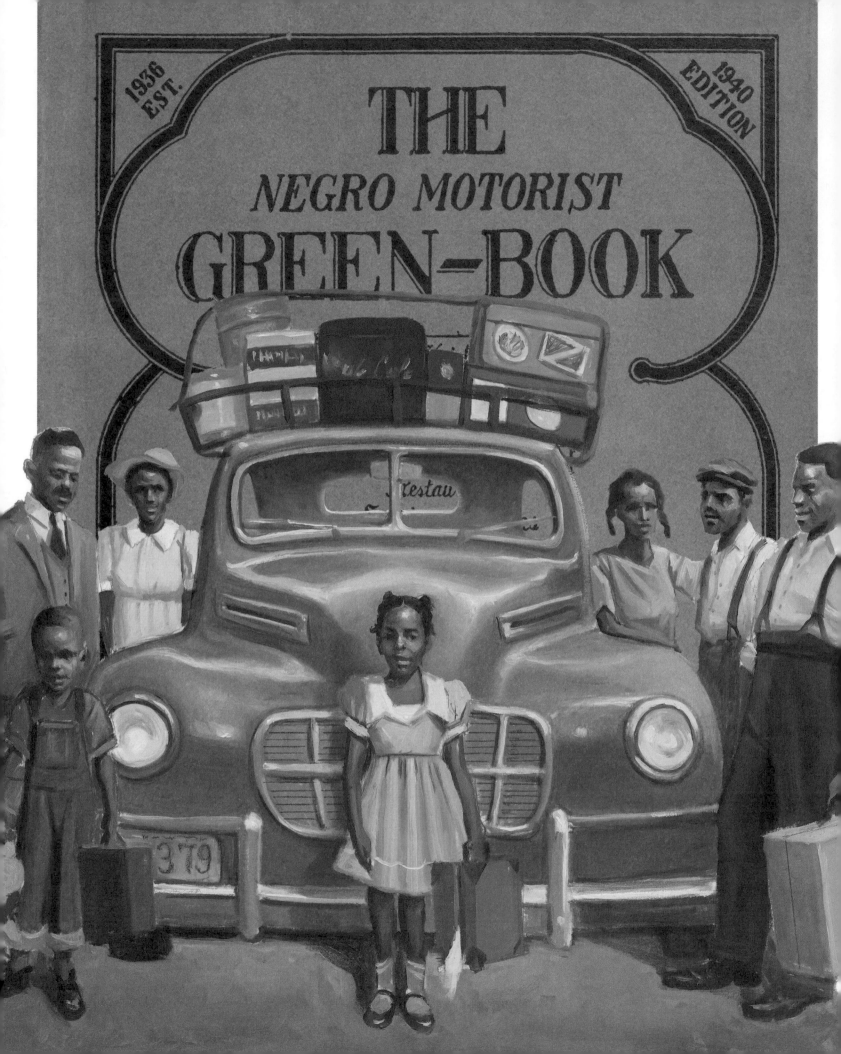

In 1940, the forty-eight-page *Green Book* listed places in the District of Columbia and in big cities in every US state.

The *Green Book* now covered far more than friendly places to lodge and dine.
It listed welcoming places to
get a new hairdo or a tailored suit,
places to get an oil change or a tire fixed,
places for tapping feet
and snapping fingers to some beats.

PLEASE MENTION "THE GREEN BOOK"

THE TALK OF THE TOWN WHEN IN NEW YORK

LITTLE ALPHA SERVICE

ONE OF NEW YORK
PIONEER CLEANER
WHERE SERVICE IS
A SMILE.

84 West 120th St.
Cor Lenox Ave.

200 WEST 136th St.
Cor. 7th Ave.

Phone: AU. 3-0671

6-8 H

ICE—R. E. EUBANKS, MGR.

BEAUTY PARLOR
Bee's—202 West
Josephine's—202
Myers & Griffi
Your Pal—222
National—301
Frances—2446
Cottie's—165
Neuway—143
Millicent—301
A. L. Smith
Oneda's—231
Sibley's—301
Edna''s—75
Beard's—325

AUT

MOTOR TUNE

Speedway
31 Dykeman St.

BARBER SHOPS

WELL

THE NEGRO TRAVE
uide to Trav
R H. GREEN,

IN THIS ISS
.... 5   Tr
.... 11   Sigh
.... 36   Trav
cation Section,

NDEX

New Yo
New Ham
New Mexi
Nevada ....
North Caro ....
Ohio ....
Oklahoma ....
Oregon ....
Pennsylvania ....
Rhode Island ....
South Carolina
South Dakota
Tennessee
Texas
Utah
Vermont
Virginia
Washington (State)
West Virginia
Wisconsin
Wyoming
Alaska
Canada
Bermuda
Mexico
aribbean
20
21
21
22
22
24
25
26
26
27
28
9

[The *Green Book*] is due off the press next month and will list 3,500 places throughout the country, all of the leading Negro newspapers, schools, and colleges, and will contain some information about the new cars.
—*The New York Age*, April 13, 1946

blished yearly by Victor H.
30, N. Y. ADVERTISING
Dec. 1. We reserve the
nform to our standards.
25 post paid; Foreign
S: send 9c, first class,
by Victor H. Green.

Elks
Avenue.
m Hollywood—100
130 Madison Ave.

29

Hack. 2-9733
FIVE POINT SERVICE STATION
Walter Levin, Prop.

BUY AT THE
ESSO
SIGN

SERVICE SUPREME
First St. and Hackensack
Ameri...

People snatched up the *Green Book* at newsstands,
in bookshops,
in libraries.

They ordered it by mail.

Esso gas stations happily carried the *Green Book* too.

And the glorious *Green Book* kept growing, growing, growing!

The Negro Motorist
GREEN BOOK
Covering The United States Like a Blanket

In 1951—a special edition on traveling by train.

In 1953—a special edition on traveling by plane.

By then, the *Green Book* was catering to folks eager to travel outside the States to, say, Canada.

Maybe Mexico too.

Also, by then, enterprising Victor Hugo Green had his own travel agency.

◆◆◆

Yes! We Can Arrange Your Vacation . . . . .
Everywhere In The United States

CRUISES — TOURS — TICKETS

WEST INDIES   CALIFORNIA   MEXICO
BERMUDA   EUROPE   CANADA
AFRICA   SOUTH AMERICA

NO SERVICE CHARGE

VICTOR H. GREEN & CO.
200 WEST 135th STREET — Room 215-A — NEW YORK 30, N.Y.

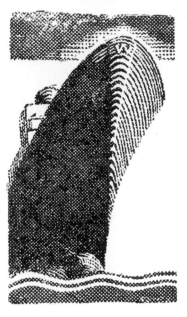

◆◆◆

While growing his book, Victor Hugo Green,
with his great get-up-and-go,
was still going one, two, and more days a week
across the Hudson River
to deliver mail in little Leonia.
That is, until . . . his retirement was
announced in the Big Apple's *Sunday News* on
a winter's day in 1953.

SUNDAY NEWS

RETIRED MAILMAN GOES
TO WORK ON HIS OWN

Green Book

ESTABLISHED
1936

Carry Your
Green Book
With You
You May
Need It.

A Classified
Motorist & Tourist Guide
COVERING THE UNITED STATES & ALASKA

1948
Edition
75¢

Folks in little Leonia, said the paper, had sent him off
into retirement with gifts:
cash ($436),
a gold watch,
plus a traveling bag!

"Now I can spend all my time getting out my annual
Negro travel guide," said Victor Hugo Green.

It was five years later, in the "Travel Whirl" column of the *New York Age*'s travel section, "Going Places!," that Alfredo Graham wrote of Victor Hugo Green as being the problem-solving type. Graham also told readers that in producing his book, Victor Hugo Green had himself been going places: "To date he has the distinction of visiting every state in the Union."

What's more, Victor Hugo Green constantly kept tabs on sites, especially hotels, "because he insists that only first-rate places deserve a listing in the *Green Book*."

25th ANNIVERSARY
1961 EDITION
The TRAVELERS'
GREEN
BOOK

reen
INTERNATIONAL
EDITION
1963-64
ut aggravation
$1.95

DE FOR
L & VACATIONS
$1.25

As much as Victor Hugo Green loved his book, he yearned for the day
when it would no longer be needed,
when ugly, hateful signs came down,
when all across America,
hotels and motels,
inns,
cottages,
campsites,
cafés,
diners,
and fancy-fine restaurants
welcomed everyone.
The day sundown towns ceased to be.

WHITE
CUSTOMERS
ONLY!

BINGO
TONITE!

COLORED
WAITING ROOM

WAITING

NO
dogs
colored
Mexicans
Jews
Irish

EASE THE SQUEEZE
RIDE THE BUS

Victor Hugo Green did not live to see that day. He died in 1960. But four years later, on July 2, 1964, millions of people—in their homes, at their jobs, on the road—celebrated the dawning of that day Victor Hugo Green had longed to see.

Owing to speeches, boycotts, marches, and other acts of activism on the part of adults and young people over the years, and the efforts of President Lyndon B. Johnson, America had a mighty civil rights bill.

The Civil Rights Act of 1964 outlawed many terrible things. One was the unjust treatment of people who, by train, by plane, by motorbike, by ship, by boat, by bus, by camper, by car, were going places.

Were Victor Hugo Green alive, surely he would have flashed a big ole sunshine smile.

There will be a day sometime in the near future when this guide will not have to be published. That is when we as a race will have equal opportunities and privileges in the United States. It will be a great day for us to suspend this publication for then we can go wherever we please, and without embarrassment. But until that time comes we shall continue to publish this information for your convenience each year.

—Victor Hugo Green in the 1948 *Green Book*

TIMELINE

November 9, 1892

Victor Hugo Green is born in New York City.

1913

Victor Hugo Green becomes a mail carrier.

June 30, 1918

Supply Sergeant Victor Hugo Green, serial number 1768215, leaves Hoboken, New Jersey, aboard a troop transport ship, the USS *President Grant*, bound for France. He is a member of the 350th Field Artillery Regiment of the US Army's heroic all-Black 92nd Division.

February 16, 1919

Victor Hugo Green returns from Brest, France, aboard the USS *Maui*.

1920

Victor and Alma live in Little Ferry, New Jersey, on Treptow Street. They will later live in Hackensack, on Union Street and on State Street.

1930

The Greens' Harlem address is 580 St. Nicholas Avenue (near 139th Street). They will later live at 938 St. Nicholas Avenue (near 157th Street).

1936

Victor Hugo Green publishes the first *Green Book* with George S. Smith, also a postal worker.

1941

After America enters World War II in December, Green suspends publication of the *Green Book*. He will resume it in 1946.

April 13, 1946

The *New York Age* publishes a photograph of Victor Hugo Green with James A. "Billboard" Jackson, a Black public relations and marketing executive with white-owned Standard Oil, parent company of Esso (now ExxonMobil) gas stations. Jackson is signing a contract for the purchase of five thousand copies of the *Green Book*, to be distributed at Esso stations. As gas stations go, Esso is in the forefront of welcoming Black customers, happily employing Black people, and allowing them to have franchises.

1947

After years of working in his and Alma's apartment, Green has office space at 200 West 135th Street, room 215-A.

1949

The *Green Book* advertises Victor's travel agency.

1959
Alma Duke Green is editor and publisher of the *Green Book* and remains so through the 1962 edition.

October 16, 1960
Victor Hugo Green dies at age 67, in a veterans hospital in lower Manhattan, and is buried in Hackensack, New Jersey.

July 2, 1964
President Lyndon B. Johnson signs into law the Civil Rights Act of 1964. It reads in part: "All persons shall be entitled to the full and equal enjoyment of the goods, services, facilities, and privileges, advantages, and accommodations of any place of public accommodation . . . without discrimination or segregation on the ground of race, color, religion, or national origin."

1966
The last *Green Book* is published by Langley Waller and Mel Tapley, both of whom had careers at the *New York Amsterdam News*. Waller and Tapley had also been copublishers of the 1963–64 editions.

March 1978
Alma Duke Green dies at age 88.

A BIT MORE ABOUT
Victor Hugo Green

Victor Hugo Green, apparently named after the famous French writer, was the oldest of three children born to William and Alice Green, both natives of Virginia. At one point in the early 1900s, when the family lived in Harlem, Victor's father was a janitor. Later, when the family lived on State Street in New Barbadoes (renamed Hackensack in 1921), Mr. Green was a janitor at the post office. Perhaps that's how Victor got a job as a mail carrier, a rare job for a Black person to hold in the early twentieth century.

NOTES

2 **"tall, well-built, always impeccably groomed":** *The Negro Travelers' Green Book.* (New York: Victor H. Green & Co., 1956), p. 6.

2 **"not only believed . . .":** Alfredo Graham, "Travel Whirl," *New York Age,* August 23, 1958, p. 33.

8 **"Hence, all Negroes . . .":** George S. Schuyler, "Traveling Jim Crow," *The American Mercury,* August 1930, p. 432.

9 **Augusta Savage in Harlem:** The Floridian moved there in the early 1920s, and that's where she later opened Savage Studio of Arts and Crafts (initially at 163 West 143rd Street, then at 239 West 135th).

9 **Langston Hughes in Harlem:** In the late 1920s and 1930s, Hughes was based at one point at 66 St. Nicholas Place, at another at 634 St. Nicholas Avenue. From 1948 until his death in 1967, his home was a brownstone at 20 East 127th Street. In 2016, author Renée Watson established here the I, Too Arts Collective, named in honor of a most beloved Hughes poem: "I, Too."

9 **Edward Kennedy "Duke" Ellington in Harlem:** From the late 1920s through 1939, this Washingtonian lived at 381 Edgecombe Avenue.

9 **Dr. May Edward Chinn in Harlem:** This first Black woman graduate of today's NYU School of Medicine and the first Black woman MD to intern at Harlem Hospital lived at 44 Edgecombe Avenue.

9 **Thurgood Marshall in Harlem:** The Baltimore native, who became the first US Supreme Court Justice in 1967, lived for a time at 409 Edgecombe Avenue, one of Harlem's swankiest apartment buildings.

12 **"WE CATER TO WHITE TRADE ONLY":** Sign in the window of a restaurant in Lancaster, Ohio, photographed in August 1938, Library of Congress Prints and Photographs Division, www.loc.gov/pictures/resource/fsa.8a17588. Last accessed July 17, 2019.

13 **"No Coloreds After Dark":** James W. Loewen, *Sundown Towns: A Hidden Dimension of American Racism* (New York: The New Press, 2018), p. 222.

18 **Black travel guides before the *Green Book*:** One was the short-lived *Hackley & Harrison's Hotel and Apartment Guide for Colored Travelers: Board, Rooms, Garage Accommodations, Etc. in 300 Cities in the United States and Canada.* It first appeared in 1930.

23 **"[The *Green Book*] is due off the press . . .":** "Standard Oil Agent Purchases Guide Books," *New York Age,* April 13, 1946, p. 3.

26 **"Yes! We Can Arrange Your Vacation . . .":** *The Negro Travelers' Green Book: Airline Edition.* (Leonia, NJ, and New York: Victor H. Green & Co., 1953), p. 13.

27–28 **"Retired Mailman . . ." and "Now I can spend . . .":** *Sunday News,* January 4, 1953, Passaic-Bergen Section, p. 2.

30–31 **"To date he has the distinction . . . in the *Green Book*.":** Alfredo Graham, "Travel Whirl," *New York Age,* August 23, 1958, p. 33.

35 **"There will be a day . . .":** *The Negro Motorist Green Book* (New York: Victor H. Green & Co., 1948), p. 1.

36 **The Greens' marriage license:** Ancestry.com. New York, NY, Marriage License Indexes, 1907-2018 [database on-line]. Lehi, UT, USA: Ancestry.com Operations, Inc., 2017.

36 **The start of Victor Hugo Green's USPS career:** PR. "The Green Book: The Forgotten Story of One Carrier's Legacy Helping Others Navigate Jim Crow 's Highways," *The Postal Record,* September 2013, pp. 22–25, www.nalc.org/news/the-postal-record/2013 /september-2013/document/09-2013_green-book.pdf. Last accessed July 17, 2019.

36 **Victor Hugo Green's deployment to and from France:** Ancestry.com. US, Army Transport Service, Passenger Lists, 1910–1939 [database on-line]. Lehi, UT, USA: Ancestry.com Operations, Inc., 2016.

36 **The Greens' addresses in New Jersey and New York City:** Ancestry.com. 1920 United States Federal Census [database on-line]. Provo, UT, USA: Ancestry.com; Operations, Inc., 2010. Images reproduced by FamilySearch, Ancestry.com. 1930 United States Federal Census [database on-line]. Provo, UT, USA: Ancestry.com; Operations Inc, 2002, and Ancestry.com. 1940 United States Federal Census [database on-line]. Provo, UT, USA: Ancestry.com Operations, Inc., 2012.

37 **Victor Hugo Green's death:** "Services Held Victor Green," *Amsterdam News,* October 22, 1960, p. 4.

37 **"All persons shall be entitled to . . .":** Transcript of Civil Rights Act (1964), Our Documents, www.ourdocuments.gov/doc .php?flash=false &doc=97&page=transcript. Last accessed July 17, 2019.

SELECTED SOURCES

*Suitable for young readers

Boyd, Herb. "Victor H. Green and His Indispensable 'Green Book,'" *Amsterdam News*, April 14, 2016, www.amsterdamnews.com/news/2016/apr/14/victor-h-green-and-his-indispensable-green-book.

"The Green Book: The Forgotten Story of One Carrier's Legacy Helping Others Navigate Jim Crow's Highways," *The Postal Record*, September 2013, pp. 22–25, www.nalc.org/news/the-postal-record/2013/september-2013/document/09-2013_green-book.pdf.

"January New Car Sales at Key Points Show Gain Over First Month of January 1932," *Detroit Free Press*, February 12, 1933.

Kennedy, Richard A. "Automobility, Hospitality, African American Tourism, and Mapping Victor H. Green's Negro Motorist Green Book." Master's Thesis, East Carolina University, 2013, www.thescholarship.ecu.edu/handle/10342/4210.

Ramsey, Calvin Alexander. *The Green Book: A Play*. Middletown, DE: Calvin A. Ramsey, 2010.

*Ramsey, Calvin Alexander with Gwen Strauss. *Ruth and the Green Book,* illustrated by Floyd Cooper. New York: Carolrhoda Books, 2013.

Rhodes, David and Daniel Stelter. "How Automakers Accelerated Out of the Great Depression," BCG.com, February 16, 2010, www.bcg.com/publications/2010/growth-automakers-accelerated-out-great-depression.aspx.

Schomburg Center for Research in Black Culture, Manuscripts, Archives and Rare Books Division, the New York Public Library. *The Negro Travelers' Green Book*, vols. 1937–57, New York Public Library Digital Collections. https://digitalcollections.nypl.org/search/index?utf8=%E2%9C%93&keywords=The+Negro+Travelers%27+Green+Book#.

Taylor, Candace. *Overground Railroad: The Green Book and the Roots of Black Travel in America*. New York: Abrams Press, 2020.

Thomas, Audrey. "Recreation without Humiliation: The Preservation of Travel Guide Resources in Portsmouth, Virginia." Thesis, Appalachian State University, 2015, www.getd.libs.uga.edu/pdfs/thomas_audrey_e_201805_mhp.pdf.

Places You Can Learn More About
THE GREEN BOOK

👉 The New York Public Library's Schomburg Center for Research in Black Culture has digitized twenty-one editions of the *Green Book*. You can check them out here: https://digitalcollections.nypl.org/collections/the-green-book#/?tab=filterResources.

👉 The Hagley Museum and Library has a copy of the 1946 edition of the *Green Book* (which the NYPL does not). You can find it here: https://digital.hagley.org/RPAM_20180325#page/1/mode/2up.

👉 At the New York Public Library's website Navigating the Green Book (https://publicdomain.nypl.org/greenbook-map), you can make pretend trips with different editions of the book.

For Zakai Eliza Lee Brunson
–T.B.

For all those brave African American souls who have
traveled throughout America, with the simple hope of
arriving safely at their destination free of trauma or terror.
–E.V.

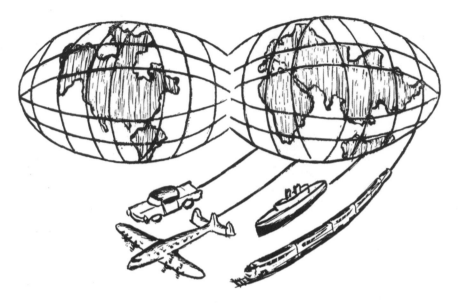

We are tremendously grateful to the wonderful HarperCollins team that worked
so hard on this book: our editor, Karen Chaplin; copy editor, Shona McCarthy;
art director, Rachel Zegar; and everyone else who helped with this book.
Tonya also thanks her sister, Nelta, and her agent, Jennifer Lyons, for their
feedback on early drafts—and for their overall support.

Quill Tree Books is an imprint of HarperCollins Publishers.

Going Places: Victor Hugo Green and His Glorious Book
Text copyright © 2022 by Tonya Bolden
Illustrations copyright © 2022 by Eric Velasquez
Map on pages 28–29 courtesy of Library of Congress, Geography and Map Division
All rights reserved. Manufactured in Italy.
No part of this book may be used or reproduced in any manner whatsoever
without written permission except in the case of brief quotations embodied in critical
articles and reviews. For information address HarperCollins Children's Books,
a division of HarperCollins Publishers, 195 Broadway, New York, NY 10007.
www.harpercollinschildrens.com

Library of Congress Control Number: 2021951272
ISBN 978-0-06-296740-4

The artist used oil paint on prepared watercolor
paper to create the illustrations for this book.
Typography by Rachel Zegar
23 24 25 26   RTLO   10 9 8 7 6 5 4 3 2
❖
First Edition